SHE'S UNSTOPPABLE

HOW I GOT IT TOGETHER AFTER
EVERYTHING FELL APART

Micah Byrd

SHE'S UNSTOPPABLE

"All scripture references are taken from the New Living Translations Version unless otherwise noted."

Micah Byrd
PO BOX 2307 Stockbridge, Ga 30281
770.573.4125
E info@micahbyrd.com
www.shesunstoppable.net

Cover design by Designer: KINGDOM GRAPHICA
ISBN: 978-1-941749-56-2
Library of Congress Catalog Number: 2016948177
FIRST EDITION: SEPTEMBER 2016

Editor: Shavonna Bush
Formatting: Coach Laura Brown
Publisher: 4-P Publishing

DEDICATION

I dedicate this book to my grandmother Carrie Lee Porter and my mother Vera Gail Odom, from whom I learned how being a woman is the most powerful position a human can assume, and how when life presents itself with challenges and transitions that although you may have fallen down you never stay down. I learned what true strength really is, and how to make good choices, be humble, grateful, and give thanks to God and the people who have helped me along the way, and appreciate the finer things in life. Also, to all the women, who are EntrepreneuHERs, wives, mothers, daughters, sisters, aunties, and girlfriends, NEVER GIVE UP. It is because of us, perseverance, persistence, and purpose is a powerful force that is not to be reckoned with.

SPECIAL THANKS

First and always, I'd like to give thanks to GOD. To my husband Todd Byrd, the love of my life and an honorable, patient man who believes in my dreams, commits to being my partner in my success, takes the good with the bad and gives me strength and confidence to take risks knowing he'll be there to catch me if I fall. To my adult children Kendra, Kayla and Kamaron, and my grandchildren Jr., and Madyson Kay, this book is for you; it is the beginning of our legacy.

To my dearest friends, who supported me emotionally, spiritually, and financially, who encouraged me to keep my dreams alive; and advised me on many matters, both large and small, I LOVE you all from the top of my heart, and I would have never accomplished this dream without each of your support.

CONTENTS

Foreword

I admire women who are strong, smart, hardworking, innovative and don't complain. Hell, I consider myself to be in this category. I am always enthused by women who are driven by their unwavering belief system. Growing up in the 80's as a young girl on the southwest side of Atlanta, Georgia, I have always been surrounded by strong women – my mother, grandmother, my mother's friends, teachers and counselors who shaped my outlook on life and encouraged my EntrepreneuHER dreams. They've supported me despite various obstacles I've faced in business but still guided me to achieve the impossible.

I knew wholeheartedly that my life was destined for success. I just didn't know how my life and love for success would translate because understanding life was not my primary focus. I didn't seek to try to figure out who I was before life started happening to me. I honestly was going to let it all take its course, and I would figure it out along the way. I was just clueless. I had no idea that planning for success was possible to accomplish.

This mindset didn't help me because I wasn't thinking about college until my junior year in high school because the topic of college wasn't discussed in my home. I did not know it was an option for me until my stepdad came into my life. The fact remains, some of the most successful people have very little primary or secondary educational training. But, what they do have are my 3P's:

purpose, **preparation,** and **perseverance**. So, growing up I knew my purpose early on. I discovered my preparation and equipped myself with perseverance along the way.

I also faced many moments of not knowing my love language. I didn't know how to express and received love. You see, I knew I was loved, but because it was never said, I was confused. I now know that when you want someone to know how you feel about them, you do two things express it and reveal it. You don't leave an opportunity open where they are guessing. In my home, the love language was expressed with gifts. My mother is an excellent gift giver. She really takes her time picking the right gifts; they always have some symbolic meaning to them, and they are always fashionable. It's a little joke in my family about giving me "cheesy" cheap gifts. I often won't accept them. It's not that they have to be expensive, just meaningful to me as the receiver and have a sense of my character within them. However, it is important to me now to have more of a meaningful connection with my family, loved ones and friends so, giving me gifts isn't the direct pathway to my heart, it's a start, but I look for authentic and honest relationships that convey their time, talents and support. I am aware that people's first perception of me is misconceived as it relates to money. I am so much more than the external. I do like the finer things in life, but the interior of my core is in-depth with peace, patience, and giving.

I remember praying one time that the need for money would not be the primary connection for people to me. I want only truthful, honest and loyal people in my circle because there have been times where I have witnessed people only wanting to get what they wanted from me. It looks ugly! I am that woman who will place both of my hands on the table. I have no regrets. I have nothing to hide.

What I admire about myself is my ability to continue forward even during my challenges and or experiences. A normal person would give up, but I just keep getting up for more. I am unique. And, because I recognized my uniqueness as a person those life experiences can't keep me stagnant. I discovered my why. Every since I found my **WHY**, I comprehend the importance of telling my **mess** through my **message.** Being transparent is not for you; it's for the other individual that needs to be encouraged to survive and never quit. Throughout my book, you will read my life challenges and experiences. There are some funny moments, that will help you realize *"How I got it together after everything fell apart"* even up to this very moment. Allow my past, present, and future to encourage, empower and motivate you to never give up on yourself

Fabulous love,

Micah Byrd

CHAPTER 1

SHE IS WHO

With all of her failures and doubts, she continues on despite them. She is who? The scripture says 1 "She is more precious than rubies." 2"She is clothed with strength and dignity, and she laughs without fear of the future." All this time when I would think about the biblical scripture of the "virtuous woman" I did not relate myself to this lady. But, as I matured and started to appreciate my character I was able to see the resemblance. In the dictionary, the meaning of virtue (n.) is moral excellence;

---

[1] Proverbs 31 v 10
[2] Proverbs 31 v 25

an admirable quality. WOW! Because many times I have been fearful of pushing forward, but I am known for trying anyway. My exterior appears to show no fear and I display a confident demeanor but within are all sorts of emotions and feeling that I am processing. My zodiac sign is Sagittarius. It is said that a Sagittarius woman is vivacious, funny, self-assured, and sophisticated. It also says that if I traveled as a child, I would need to continue this throughout my adult life. I know this to be true because I am adventurous. I am a woman that needs a challenge and intellectual stimulation in all aspects of my life.

I know you are wondering why I'm sharing this information with you. Well, I learned a long time ago my outlook on life begins with knowing who and whose I am. I am positive and optimistic about life, it makes me highly successful at what I set out to do. I can convert into an introvert. I am intellectually stimulating, and the struggle to keep up with me is a challenge because I am a smart woman who seeks to understand *my* **mess**, in an effort to share the **message** for God's **missions**. I am always challenging and testing my ability to endure. I wholeheartedly step out on faith without a net. I am a risk-taker and doing so has rewarded me with experiences and stories which are first for my immediate family. As I think about these experiences, I now fully understand that they were the roadmap to my now.

There have been many times where I questioned GOD. I thought he had it out for me. I would ask, "why me"? And, I would receive an immediate response "why not you"? I can always hear GOD speak to me when I am questioning him. I believe that I hear him speaking to me in the beginning of my experience. I have doubts because when I was a young girl, I didn't trust nor believe in myself. And, I can't recall any early experiences where I was assured nor confirmed in my abilities and aspirations. I just had to dig deep and believe in myself knowing that I have been equipped and destined for this life.

Hearing GOD's response is mind blowing. I

know many of you gorgeous ladies have lived and learned a thing or two, so I'm sure you've heard the saying, "If you want to make GOD laugh, just tell him your plans." Now let's get started.

SHE'S UNSTOPPABLE 101

My age was thirteen, and I was just entering high school. I attended the illustrious Frederick Douglas High School in Atlanta, Georgia. In August 1984, I walked into the homeroom of Ms. G. Miller, the English teacher. Ms. Miller was encouraging and different all at the same time. She had no idea how she impacted my life. She was of Caribbean decent, and you could hear the accent coming from her voice as she called the roll. We were so silly back then, we would laugh every time she called the roll. We didn't know how blessed we were to have before us someone who could expand our mind and increase our territory without leaving our very own state.

SHE'S UNSTOPPABLE 102

My first day of school was a horrible experience. I was so nervous being a freshman, affectionately called a subfreshmen by the upperclassmen at this large high school. There were so many new faces. I remember walking down the hall looking lost and lonely. I was unsure where my first class was, and the upperclassmen could smell the fear. They took advantage of it too. They would send you to floors where they knew your next class was not located. There were so many things going on in my head. I had a lot to remember like, don't talk to boys, be to class on time, and don't get into trouble.

However, I was sure of one thing; I knew I was sharp! I had my own style. It was very modern, chic and girly. My mother is a well-dressed woman, which is where I get it from naturally. I have always had an eye for aesthetics and patterns. I just didn't realize that this was one of my many gifts, and I certainly didn't know what to do with it.

It was the fall of 1987, right before my high-school boyfriend was to leave to go to college. He was headed off to Alcorn State in Lorman, Mississippi. The place was set to be extremely boring, yet viable for his potential career. He was incredibly talented in sports, and I had high hopes for him and us because we knew we were going to be lifelong partners.

He was preparing to leave in the next few days, so he came to my house late one evening. This day sticks out so vividly in my mind, almost too clear. My emotions were high because we knew that it was going to be a while before we would see each other again. We didn't know how long but we knew it would be a while before we would see each other again. He was raised from a humble upbringing and his life was much different from how I was raised. But, our feelings were intense; you could touch me and the tingling sensation would take hold. I knew something was going down that night because every woman knows when she is going to give it up. We lived in a very affluent area in the Southside of Atlanta and directly behind our condo unit was a lake with ducks. On this particular night, we decided to go out to the lake to talk and kiss. We had already been sexually active but this particular night was different because in our hearts we knew that it was time for him to leave, and we both were sad about having to part ways. In my young and tender heart, I thought this guy was it for me. He was my gentle giant, and I thought that we would be together forever. He was scary to most, but to me, he was the most humble guy I had ever had a close encounter with as a teenager. He provided security, fun and genuine love. There were some things I did as a teenager with him that I was never exposed too. My mother was strict with me and looking back I am appreciative.

On this beautiful night, it was going to happen. It did too. We had sex and for some reason, I immediately knew that I felt different afterward. I felt that it was the turning point in my life that I had no knowledge of at the time. The one that my mother had warned me of. I want to believe, even now, if there were more discussions about my options and the opportunities that were available to me that perhaps my path would have been different. But, who would know my story better than God?

SHE'S UNSTOPPABLE because...

SHE is her own cheerleader!

SHE'S UNSTOPPABLE 103

Let's fast-forward to June 1988, I was nine months pregnant and my life was moving faster than Superwoman. It was happening before my eyes, it was something that I thought would only be visible in a book. Oops! It was going down in less than a month; my life became pretty hectic. I got married on June 4th. I graduated on June 10th, my baby shower was June 11th and my first child was born on June 27th. Instantly, I was a young wife, mother and a high school graduate at the coming age of 18. I also received my acceptance letter to Spelman College. The one thing my peers didn't know. There was a lot going on and it was happening fast.

I was ecstatic about the new me; although I was apprehensive about how it looked. I had this opportunity to attend this prestigious institution but my current experience had me not feeling worthy of such award. The experience of being a new wife, and young mother. Because during those days, there was a huge stigmatism about young mothers. If my experiences were different at the time I would have jumped at the opportunity to start school in the fall. I choose to delay my entrance; a year in a half later as a non-traditional student.

I was able to matriculate through for two years right before having my second child. My step-father's joke about me was, "I was having a baby every Saturday night." After giving birth to my second daughter, a decision about my life had to be made. At this time my marriage was taking me through challenges that I had not imagined would happen such as infidelity and criminal activities that created an unsafe environment for the kids and me. So, I opted to start working a full-time job at Lanier Worldwide, a company my mother had worked for nearly eighteen years before I started. It began my career as a young accountant. I started as an Inventory accounting clerk, and I was good at it too. I am visual learner so this field came natural, me understanding numbers and comprehending debits and credits. It just clicked. I enjoyed working, but there were challenges. It felt like overnight I was a wife, mother, and student and now somewhere trying to care for me and my children.

My mom and I would ride to work together and would eat lunch in her office. I was beginning to feel as though I had matured into a woman. I was making significant sacrifices in my life. I temporarily suspended my educational pursuits to be an involved parent in the lives of my two girls and after doing some thorough self-evaluation regarding my future, I decided that there would be another chance for me to finish school. With all the guilt and shame behind me, I was able to persevere forward and prepare for my future.

SHE'S UNSTOPPABLE because...

SHE *is not fooled by those experiences dressed up as distractions because she knows "life is 10% of what happens to her and 90% of what she does about it!"*

SHE'S UNSTOPPABLE 104

As I matured at being a mother, wife, and employee, life provided another set of experiences for me. I was faced with making the choice of divorcing my high school love or continuing in a marriage that brought me nothing but pain and sadness.

It was a difficult decision because I had two young girls and I was still growing myself. The damage of infidelity, a love child, broken trust and the realization that I had out-grown that marriage was my answer.

We quickly realized that we were better at parenting than being married. There was a lot of pain within my marriage. I had to hear that my husband thought our second child wasn't his. It was an embarrassment and also damaging to my character. If nothing else, I am faithful and loyal to those I love. I never understood why this man who knew me better than anyone else would say such hurtful things. What exactly did I have to gain from pinning a child on him that wasn't his? He didn't have any money; he wasn't famous, and he barely would pay the child support payment without taking legal actions against him to do so. The divorce turned into a legal separation because he wanted to play before paying and I honestly didn't have the energy nor resources to fight that battle at the time. It was just another reminder that I was so far away from truly knowing and exercising my true potential. The day would come where I would settle all my unfinished business. So, I went on with my life, temporarily.

I thought my soul was healed and began dating a year later. I met this guy who has similar looks as my first husband. I knew him from the Mechanicsville area, where I would visit with my mother when she visited her girlfriend. Hindsight should have told me to run for the hills. But, I was just shy of being 22 years old and extremely naive. He was a decent guy. He was affectionate, kind and a hustler just like my first husband. In the beginning, he provided a life of adventure. I was the straight and narrow one in that relationship. I went to work every day from 9 to 5. I provided more of the reliable and stable environment for my daughters.

Finally, the day came, and the unfinished business with my first husband was resolved. He signed the divorce papers. I was so happy to be able to move forward with my life. It was a significant change for me because the support order increased and he began to step up as a father should for the girls. I could once and for all completely move on with my life.

Not too long after that, I found out I was pregnant with my third child. I was as excited about this birth as I was about my other two. The relationship with my boyfriend had progressed; he had even proposed with a 2.5 carat ring. His mom and I both were surprised. I remember this day so clearly. It was raining outside, and I had just finished cleaning up from dinner with the girls. He had not made it home yet, but it was going to be late when he got there. I wasn't sure what had changed, but I was in tune enough to know that something wasn't right. This sort of late night coming home went on for a while until one day I decided that I had enough and he needed to leave. Well, that experience did not go so well because it was my first time getting into a physical altercation. It was utterly ridiculous to be at this point in my life and having to fight, especially after having my son who was the blessing from this relationship. I am very sure it was drug related. He was doing drugs. His behaviors exhibited a lot of habits that indicated some sort of substance. I couldn't prove it because it wasn't done in front of me but let's just say that things did go missing.

Having my kids and being a mother is my gift. I learned so much about me as an individual, mother, and woman. I am still learning a lot about myself daily. I learned that I am much more powerful and resourceful than I've ever given myself credit. I learned that no relationship, nor individual defines the true feeling of what I think of me.

SHE'S UNSTOPPABLE 105

This part of the **mess** I still have difficulty revealing the **message.** I have run from this part of my life for so many years that I have run right into a brick wall. I was young, somewhere around 25 or 26 years young. I had decided that after that last relationship, I was going to be single. I was going to focus on me. I wasn't going to allow the stigmatism of being a young black mother determine how I felt about myself. I was going to press right through and live. If love was to happen it would have to find me. My closest girlfriend and I started hanging out on Campbellton Road at *Marko's* and *Club 731*. I know we hung out every weekend, at least it felt that way. But my mother wasn't having that junk, keeping my kids on ever other weekend. We were regulars at the spot. I remember some good times partying in those clubs. I believe I was trying to catch up on all those house parties and afterschool functions I missed out on during high school.

One night the club was packed with people from the neighborhood. Everybody was there, even my girl's boyfriend. He was acting like he didn't see her as if he'd forgot this girl is crazy. Let's just say that our night ended early, we had to leave the club. We said our good nights. I got in my car and drove across the street to the all-night gas station to get a bottle of water and some gas. You know I needed that bottle of water, to wake my butt up or at least keep me from falling asleep while driving. As I am exiting the gas station this guy opens the door for me. I assumed he was trying to come inside. So, of course, I said thank you because on Campbellton Road it's not often that a guy would open the door. But, he said hello and asked me what was my name. I felt out of placed, one because I was there without my girl and two he was different from my usual catch. I was completely taken off-guard but I told him my name. We stood outside the gas station talking, trying to get to know each other into the AM of the next day. We exchanged numbers and so the courtship begin. We meet up for dinner not too long after meeting at the club. I couldn't help but notice that he has some physical disparities in his appearance. But, he was a nice guy. He had been employed at his job for eight years at the time. He started immediately after high school. He was the father of two boys. If my memory serves me correctly his kids were around my girl's age. We begin hanging around each other more and more as time allowed. I got a chance to find out what part of Atlanta, he was from. He grew up in the Bluff. It is the English Avenue and Vine City area. This area is around the Georgia Dome where the Atlanta Falcons play their home games. During those days it was infamous for its high crime and murder rates. I can't even remember the story he told me about what happen to his face. It did take me some time to get used to looking at him without pity or confusion showing through my eyes. What I do remember that gives me chills to this day, is he didn't have a great relationship with his mother. It stills feels strange talking about this. His relationship looked estranged to me then. I remember us driving over there one day to give her a birthday gift. He'd asked if I wanted to come up and of course, I said no. I couldn't get settled in her house there was shit everywhere. Nothing seemed like it had a real home. Besides it was nasty on the inside, and there were too many steps to climb to get to her apartment. I just didn't want to be bothered. That visit didn't last long. I was eager to leave and get back to my side of town. I would always opt out of going upstairs to her house when we would go visit. He still had not been personally and formally introduced to my kids until six months of dating. This courtship developed into a marriage of three years. It had it secrets too. He switched careers when we became a family. There were a lot of mouths to feed. He was an over-the-road truck driver. I was an active parent in my kid's life. The girls were involved in Girls Scouts, school events and sleepovers with a select group of kids. We were actively involved at our Pentecostal church, to which I was introduced to by one of his co-workers. Life seemed normal. I honestly can't remember what changed in the marriage that shifted. It just didn't seem the same, when he would come home off-the-road. The distance went on for some time. I allowed it to carry on because he was away from home during the week, and the weekends became unbearable when he was there.

Until one early morning, he came home. I woke him up immediately after he had just gotten into a deep sleep. I couldn't wait to have this conversation with him. I needed to ask him several questions, and it had to happen in person. I didn't want to alarm him about what he was going to face when he got home. I needed to find out if this was true what my daughter said to me early in the week that startled me. I was very upset. My daughter shared with me that he, the man I invited into mine and their lives, to whom I married touched her in an area that was inappropriate.

This still breaks my heart. There are times that I am sad and disappointed in myself. This behavior is disgusting and no woman, child or anyone should be subject to this type of abuse. Of course, he denied such behavior but I immediately told him he had to leave my home. Months went by and my daughter later shared with my husband Todd, further details of the inappropriateness. My daughter told my husband Todd, that she did not want to tell me before because she thought I wouldn't believe her. Hearing that hurt me to my core! The authorities were called immediately, he was arrested and later incarcerated for sexual abuse to a minor. It was a big case in the county we lived in at the time. He is ordered by law to stay and far away from me and my children. This timeframe of my life is a vague memory. I really have suppressed it so deep that it is never discussed. It is only talked about when my daughter wants to talk about it. She is healing, and she has been involved in council groups for sexually abused kids of blended families. I am still in the healing phase too. I have forgiven myself for inviting such an evil person into our lives. But, it is part of my **mess,** that important to share through the message.

SHE'S UNSTOPPABLE because...

SHE *survives!*

CHAPTER 2

LIVE TO LOVE

Were you a daddy's girl? Is being a daddy's girl ever something that you wanted to experience? I definitely wanted to know what being daddy's girl was all about. I don't recall much about my biological dad prior to him passing in my late twenties. I have very little memories of him as a little child. I often wondered if my biological dad was an active parent in my life if I would have had my previous experiences. You see my biological father was paraplegic. I was told his injuries were due to him playing street ball in Decatur, Georgia. I knew he was capable of being involved because even though he was paraplegic, he was able to get around. He had a customized van that he was able to drive, even though he always had a handler driving him.

As I aged and began having children of my own, I wanted to know more about him for myself. I believed it wouldn't hurt me to visit him and take my kids with me. Throughout my visits with my dad, I learned a lot about him. I learned he really wanted to be an active dad to me and my brother. But, he couldn't get past his own sadness of his paralysis.

I remember my last visit to see him at The Shepard Spinal Center. I was around twenty-eight. I had visited enough to muster up the courage to engage in questioning about his inability to be active in my life. It was a pretty day. I was prepared because I had written him a letter several years prior to this encounter. I had envisioned me having this opportunity of addressing him. So, I memorized what was on the letter and was determined to get a resolution that day. I told you I am a determined woman, who wants to acknowledge *my* **mess**, in hopes of inspiring others through the **message.** I wanted to make sure I got all questions answered. I was determined to leave no stone unturned. I joked around with him at first just to see what kind of mood he was in. I didn't want to upset him. I wanted him to be open to answering every question truthfully and completely because I wanted to move forward in my life. I was determined to find out if my daddy loved and cared about me.

I jumped right into asking my questions. I asked why he wasn't involved in our lives. Why wasn't he an active father even after him and my mother divorced? I was shocked that he answered his little girl's questions, candidly. My purpose in examining him was because I really wanted to know if my father loved us. I was ready to **LIVE TO LOVE.**

My first real encounter with a father began when my mother married her second husband. I knew my mom was dating him for a while before my brother and I ever had a chance to meet him. It was at a pinnacle time in my life. I was in high school; I remember somewhere around my sophomore year. His being there was a breath of fresh air. He took care of my mother. He moved us into a better community. He later asked my mother to resign from her job of 18 years to help take care of the kids. He talked to me about my plans after high school. It was the first time that I had that conversation with anyone. He cared and it showed! He wasn't perfect, but he was my Papa.

SHE'S UNSTOPPABLE 107

I learned a lot from my stepdad. He was a man of very little words, but very giving of his time. He was very instrumental in teaching me how to handle small repairs to my home. I learned that a man should support, take care and love his woman. He made sure my mother didn't want for anything. He worked hard. He had worked at *Lockheed Marteen* for 43 years before retiring. He also operated a well-known restaurant here in Atlanta, Georgia on Lee Street, called *Pilgreen's.* There's this running joke between my brother, me and the family about us believing that Papa owned the restaurant because every night he would bring home fried chicken and cauliflower for dinner. Even after I moved out on my own with the kids, I was able to go to the restaurant to get dinner for us. I finally knew what it felt like to be a daddy's girl even if I was an adult. I knew he had my best interest in mind. My kids and I didn't want for anything. While writing this book, my dad, "Papa," passed away. There were a lot of things I didn't get the chance to tell him. He wasn't in the best health when I began writing my book. I know he is proud of me just like he was when I received my undergraduate and graduate degrees.

SHE'S UNSTOPPABLE because...

*Every time **SHE** thinks about giving up on herself, she reminds herself of her **WHY**.*

The scripture says [3]"She extends a helping hand to the poor and opens her arms to the needy." [4]"Her children stand and bless her..." I am that woman who is a giver by default. I am also a woman who is suited better for marriage. I am not that type of woman who will go long periods of time dating a gentleman. This is the **NO JUDGEMENT ZONE** over here. I have been around the block a time or two.

---

[3] Proverbs 31 v 20

[4] Proverbs 31 v 28

SHE'S UNSTOPPABLE 108

My first marriage, I was young. I definitely didn't have time and knowledge to mature first. I experience was the On the Job Training (OJT), and the rest I learned from the experiences of others. I consider myself blessed to be found honorable to be asked for my hand in marriage. Although, it is better to have a life-long partnership. I cannot beat myself up over circumstances not working out. I believe that a true woman knows her value is not tied up into the idea of marriage but into the quality of the relationship.

I am married and have been married for 11 years. We were both raised in the same neighborhood. As a young girl, I knew of my husband but I didn't know him. I always thought he was much older than me until we met later on in life as adults. We tease each other about being polar opposites. Our astrological sign warns us to stay away from each other, and there's some truth to that because when it's good, it's good but, oh boy when it's bad, let's just say that we both go to our separate corners. That is because we are both driven individuals seeking to know thyself in this world. He is a great guy, very humble and soft spoken. He isn't the type of gentleman that raises his voice. He's non-confrontational, but he is a man that speaks his mind and has a lot to say because he is very intelligent. We both are two strong individuals in this marriage, and I am the one that is more stubborn than most. In any relationship, there should always be one that will raise the white flag first. Most often that isn't me; however, I am learning to live and not be so stern. The scripture says [5] "Love is patient and kind. Love is not jealous or boastful or proud or rude. It does not demand its own way. It is not irritable, and it keeps no record of being wronged. [6]It does not rejoice about injustice but rejoices whenever the truth wins out. [7] Love never gives up, never loses faith, it is always hopeful, and endures through every circumstance". This time around I finally feel like I got it right. This marriage displays everything talked about in 1 Corinthians because I opened myself up for the opportunity of **LIVING TO LOVE**. I am a

---

[5] 1 Corinthians 13 v 4
[6] 1 Corinthians 13 v 6
[7] 1 Corinthians 13 v 7

much better wife, mother, grandmother, friend, and businesswoman. But situations change and when they do you must adjust accordingly, and never quit.

I believed this to be the worst experience for any woman during the time it was happening. I noticed that my relationship with my husband began to change the past two years. There was a sudden shift when we purchased our home. Our communication towards one another instantly changed. It was harsh and felt unloving. For some time, I had a woman's intuition and it just kept nudging at me. There was nothing specific that I could put my hand on, it just didn't feel the same.

This particular day I was working in my boutique alone. All my staff associates were off for the day, and I'd remembered that the mailbox had not been checked. I go to the mailbox to get the contents, and I noticed this one strange looking letter that had my name handwritten and addressed to me. Immediately a strange feeling went all over my body. I felt some kind of way, and it had a familiar feeling. What I do know from previous experiences, is you might forgive, but often you don't ever forget. I opened the letter only to see what I wouldn't wish on an enemy if I had any. After reading the first few words, I knew it wasn't going to end well. I got lost in the sauce. I thought my marriage and relationship to my best friend was solid. I neglected and forgot that I needed to continue to nurture my marriage, as I pursue to achieve success. It should be just as important to keep a healthy relationship and marriage while balancing other things outside of my home.

In short, the letter basically stated the writer didn't want to be identified and they "were a coward to have to tell me in this way." The letter said, "I was a good woman to my husband, but he had been cheating on me for a while." WOW, what a punch to my gut! To this day I get emotional talking about it. I felt and still feel betrayed until recent events.

SIDE NOTE: *The writer never provided proof of their statements; however they did suggest that I hire a private investigator.*

Let's fast-forward to a year and a half later after receiving the heartbreaking letter. I put the letter aside after addressing my strong concerns with my husband, and his continued heartfelt expressions that he has **never** stepped out on me in our 15-year courtship.

Now don't misunderstand that to mean that I had forgiven him for the information written, just note it as there was further information to gather before I could consider giving up on my marriage from a letter with no proof provided. I needed time and space to sort things out. I had a partial feeling there might be truth to what he was saying about it being untrue. I have never personally received a phone call, nor has any woman ever approached me about infidelity with my husband. And, you know there are some ratchet women out here in "these streets" that will do the most to destroy someone's home because of what they are missing. As a woman what was I to do with that information, and no proof? I trust him, I had no prior reason not too. I knew going into to my marriage that my husband and I both are friendly people who live a colorful life; we both are business owners and have relationships with others that are of the opposite sex. I have never felt intimated nor have I ever felt like I didn't know where I stand as primary with my husband. But, receiving that letter I must admit made me feel some kind of way.

I am a confident woman, who doesn't

notice female competition among myself and another woman. Yet, I was starting to feel different after the letter. Until one night, after a date night and after the letter.

I was awakened to the buzzing of his phone. It was very unusual because normally his phone would be put away and out of sight. I immediately picked up the phone and saw a text message from [8]*skank* number 1, and to spare you the details, let's just say the message was inappropriate for any man to receive let alone a married man. Then right behind the first text message, comes another text message from *skank* number 2 and this message was the straw that started the war.

Throughout the years there have been multiple situations that I allowed to slip by because I was and have been more concerned with accomplishing and building my brands. It was important for me to work on myself and my business because for the majority of my life I had to be a mother and give any of my time at that role first. So, it was finally my time to do for me and I

---

[8] **Skank** is defined as a sleazy or unpleasant person.

almost forgot that I was married. I still needed to learn and master how to nurture that relationship all while balancing life, and success. **Girl,** I need to keep my eyes open and tend to my husband and manage to keep my marriage healthy and solid just as much as I want to accomplish building my brands.

Since this new experience, my ability to trust again has been temporarily damaged. It is difficult to be in a relationship where the trust is questionable. I do not want to nor will I manage a grown adult. In recent events, since I started the journey of exposing my mess, we were gifted a blessing with finding out who wrote the letter. God will reveal the truth to you if you just wait on him. I am still unsure why another female would write this letter, especially since neither I nor my husband knows her.

We both only met her once in our lifetime, but just imagine the damage the letter could have done to my marriage of 11 years. What we needed to do was regain our **why for** our marriage. And, as for me I will be consistent, think big, be a listener and invest in my marriage. All the things that we did when we first got married. I can't focus on why people do what they do, I must continue to focus on my family, myself and businesses. Therefore, I **will keep** putting one stiletto in front of the other.

SIDE NOTE:
See the snapshot of the text message we received from my husband's friend, who received the text message from the friend of the female who wrote the letter. She is or was a female girlfriend acquaintance of my husband's friend. I know just drama....

Micah Byrd

I'm hurt.. That she would tell these tales about me. You have managed to open my eyes. Thank You

You have no idea.. Like I told you b4 she's the one that sent your homeboy wife that letter talking about he was coming to your house with other women

Please tell me your Lying. All Joke to aside.

She told me about your son mom using your for money and you trying to build a relationship with him

Yea right.. How would I know that.

WTF!!! 😵 😵 😵

She told me about you and your wife and you being so hurt by the first one that died and that's why none of your other relationships work..

Look what I just came across

SHE'S UNSTOPPABLE

SHE'S UNSTOPPABLE because...

---

*There are times in **her** life when she feels she just can't keep going, then **she** remembers all the other times **SHE has** made it through.*

SHE'S UNSTOPPABLE LIVE TO LOVE
moments...

_____

_____

_____

_____

_____

_____

_____

_____

_____

_____

_____

_____

_____

_____

_____

_____

_____

_____

CHAPTER 3

SHE IS FABULOUS

The scripture says, [9] "She makes her own bedspreads. She dresses in fine linen and purple gowns." Before I understood my purpose and natural gifts I was fabulous. Being fabulous simply means that one is extraordinary, remarkable and exceptional in all her ways. If you think of fashion and fabulousness, you will think of me after you've met me. It just goes together, and I am not boasting, I just have a natural talent for style and the ability to pull it all together with minimum effort which makes me extraordinary. There are people that attend workshops and classes to learn about obtaining this gift. You can do the same! Allow me to share

---

[9] Proverbs 31 v 22

with you how to assume, manage and maintain being "fabulous."

My family nicknamed me "Dusty". I was the little girl that cared very little about material things but confidence exuded from me even when I was dirty from playing outside. I was a determined and driven child. There is nothing wrong with having those characteristic as a woman especially if you are a woman in business. But, if you think being a woman gives you a hall pass to have attributes that support you being aggressive, arrogant, angry and asking more of others than you give of yourself, you need to continue reading more of this book.

There is nothing worse than being that woman who is considered the "witch" because she lacks charm, charisma, and coolness in every area of her life. Yes, being a business owner is primarily male dominated, but I never display a sexual, aggressive and arrogant demeanor when I am attempting to get a contract, or interacting with my male clients. I have seen this behavior before, and it is very displeasing and disappointing to see women display this persona when in business. Being a business woman is simply a title, not a pass to display un-lady like gestures, and it doesn't make you fabulous.

What I like about the Bible's story of the **virtuous woman** is that this sister shows and possess moral standards in all her doings. She was right with her husband, her kids and the people she transacted business with. The scripture also says [10] "she finds wool and flax and busily spins it. [11] She is like a merchant's ship, bringing her food from afar." Again, being able to generate revenue from multiple ventures and keep it all together is another exceptional trait that makes you **fabulous.** Ever wondered how other successful women just seem to have it all together?

Well, don't wonder anymore. Just understand that they plan those things that are imperative to them. Successful women plan and we prepare for important things. We make sure that our family, business, and life is first and foremost in every area of our daily adventures. Now, does that mean that impromptus won't happen?

---

[10] Proverbs 31 v 13

[11] Proverbs 31 v 14

Absolutely not but when they do, you must measure their importance to the things that have already been planned and prepared.

In the book of Proverbs, this woman was described as having it all together, and being good at it all. The book goes on to describe her as an "excellent wife". What does it mean to be excellent? Excellent is a descriptive of being without fault, not perfect but willing to go through to achieve the unachievable. **SHE** is determined to beat the odds. It was never planned out for her as a little girl, so she had to make her plans on her own.

SHE'S UNSTOPPABLE because...

---

*Behind every one of her experiences, there will be a lesson and a blessing. SHE **MUST** wait on both of them.*

---

*SHE'S UNSTOPPABLE 50 fabulous
things about you ...*

_____

_____

_____

_____

_____

_____

_____

_____

_____

_____

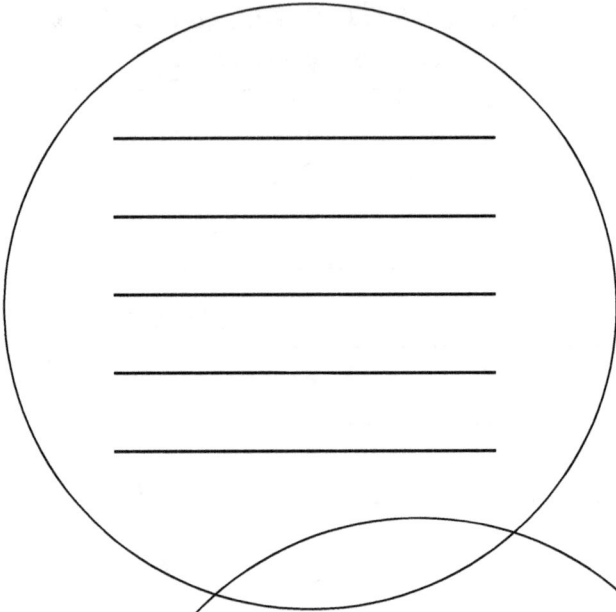

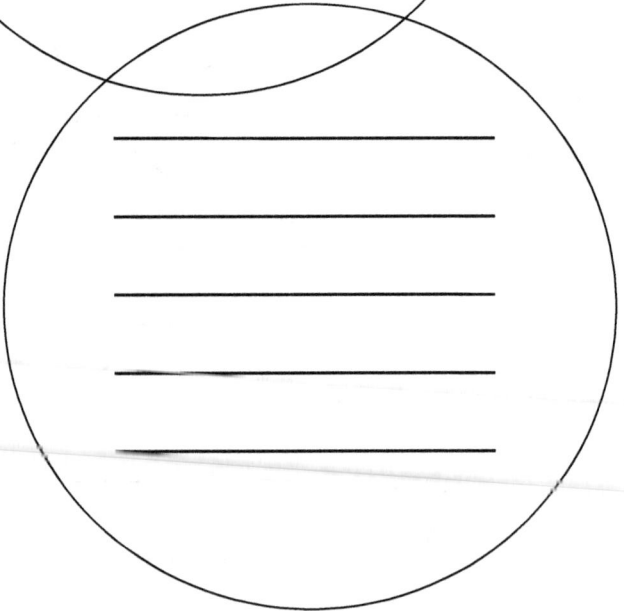

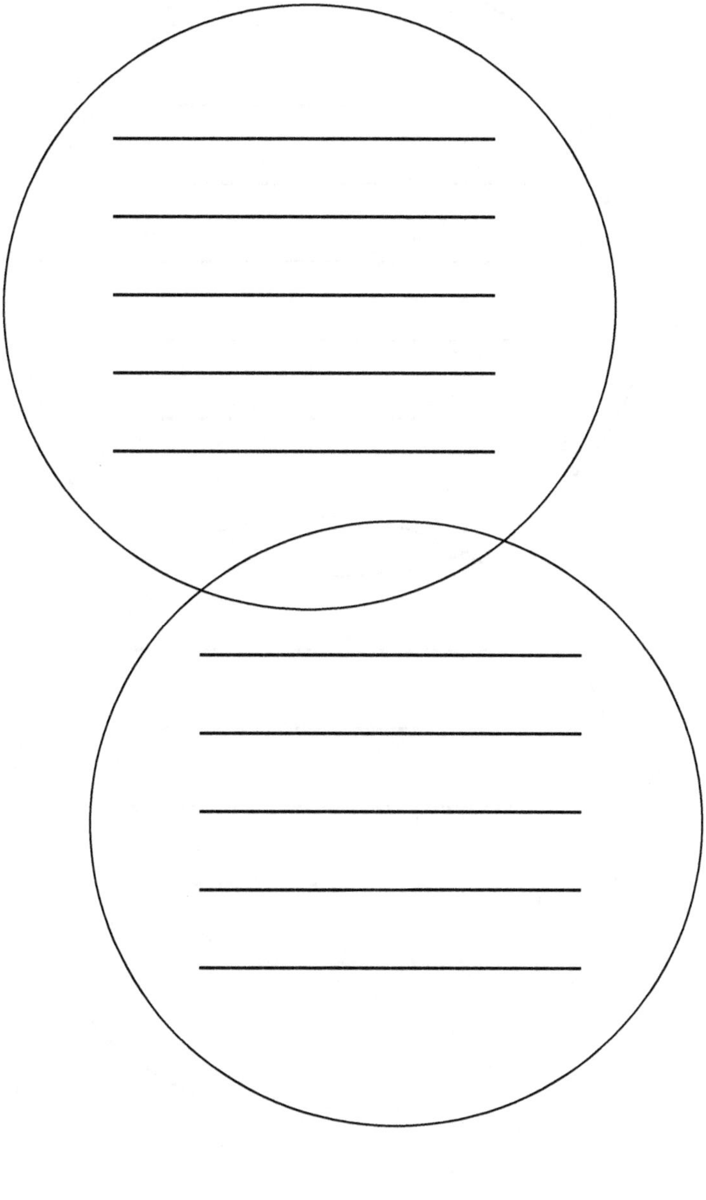

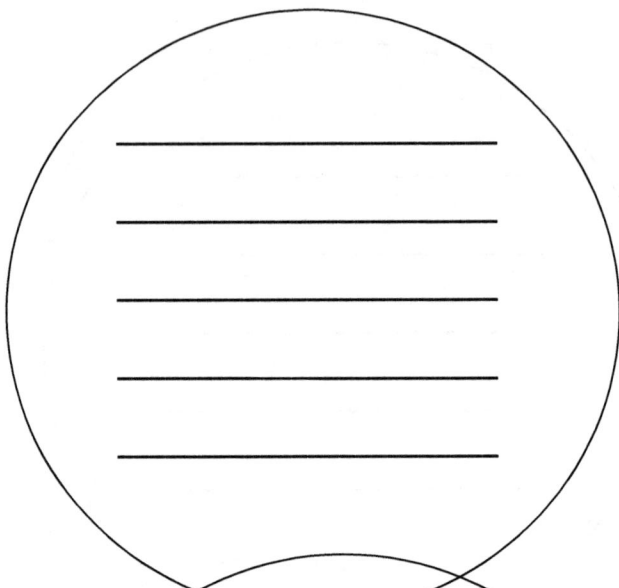

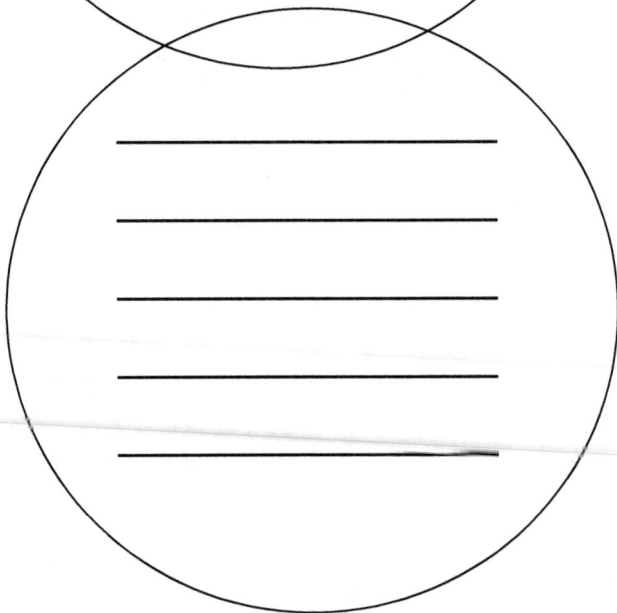

_____

_____

_____

_____

_____

_____

_____

_____

_____

_____

CHAPTER 4

SHE IS
ORGANIZED

Oh, I function much better being organized. I get excited about everything being in order because it keeps me irrefutable. The scripture says [12]"She carefully watches everything in her household and suffers nothing from laziness." I wholeheartedly believe that I am able to juggle so many roles and responsibilities because I am organized. Whenever I have not organized my thoughts, activities, assignments, and attire, I am unhinged. Jokingly, my A.D.D. kicks in! My closet, clothes, and shoes **must be** in order at all times. I mean color

---

[12] Proverbs 31 vs 27

coded and placed in the clear shoe boxes a certain way (it makes it easier to see what pair is in the box). The clothes must be hung on the hanger a particular way, and everything must go back to its original place when done using.

I secretly did a study on myself regarding my ability to manage multiple activities while being disorganized in my living arrangements. My ability to remain focused was chaotic. I couldn't keep up with my personal and business responsibilities, and I begin to allow my health and sanity to take a back seat. One day, I was driving down to South Florida for business, and I started crying like there was no tomorrow. Luckily, I was in the vehicle by myself but not alone, because it was in that quiet time that I heard my spirit say, "you must release." At the time I wasn't able to articulate the exact direction, but later I was stirred into **journaling** my thoughts. This was something that I use to do before life became so important for me to seize by the bullhorns. I physically, and mentally got caught chasing the dreams. I completely forgot that they were mine, and I didn't need to chase what was specifically designed for me. My totality has to be in sync with my mind, spirit and soul and the best way that I've accomplished this skill is keeping everything in its place. I encourage you to write down those things that need to be accomplished for the day, right before going to bed. Make it a habit! Do not make your to-do list more than five things because the more items on your daily list that aren't completed tells your psyche that you weren't successful. It is known that we as humans are instantly drawn to point out the negative in oneself instead of the positive. So, in an effort to be organized mentally and in the natural, one will need to compartmentalize their thoughts. To do so, you must **set purposeful goals.** I am persuaded that life without goals is only existing. Goals fuel you with energy, and they provide you with direction and a blueprint for your life. Not having goals will make you a victim of your circumstance and you will end up being carried to and from every distraction that comes your way.

Being a woman of organization, who lives on purpose means you must set purposeful goals. Purposeful goals are simply your dreams with a deadline. What are your "big dreams" that God has given you? You should turn these into short and long-term goals. I set both short and long-term goals for my life. My big dream from God is to teach and speak to women entrepreneuHERs about the fundamentals of business from opening to closing their doors. I have been working towards this for the past twenty-three years. My success is created as a result of creating goals that support my one big dream. Each year and mid-year I create a set of goals that helps me move towards my purpose and keeps me **organized** with my daily life. You **live** by *lists, notes, and goals,* and you **survive** by *lists, notes, and goals.* On my list are books I want to write, speaking engagements I want to speak at, mentors and social circles I need in my life and subjects that I want to master. None of these purposeful goals would be accomplished if I didn't get organized and remain organized. Once my purposeful goals are organized and written, I select a few to make my primary driving force until I have accomplished them. **It works *trust me.*** I have purposely seen many things come into fruition just by organizing and goal setting. Some goals come to pass with very little effort while others take a lot of work, but with the list(s) it helps me to remain organized, focused and encouraged until it comes to pass. I am always stretching myself to reach new goals and as a result, I live the purposeful life I inspire others to lead. You are capable of your big dream too, but it starts with an organization and purposeful goal setting.

Be mindful, it is not the goals that will define your success, but the type of person you will become in order to reach your goals by being organized. As an example, my goal to write books behind the scenes of that goal, I had to master habits such as organization, self-discipline, time management, deadline delivery, stamina, perseverance, and obtaining knowing about the book industry. I created self-discovery which aided me in creating space to write, blocking out distractions and disruptions in life, giving myself time to be creative in my writing process. I had to become an expert on the subject, which meant that I had to allow those experiences to manifest in my life for them to be authentic, relevant and encouraging content that I would be worth sharing with my readers. Then it was imperative that I stick to the book project until it was completed, all the while investing my ongoing time, resources and effort until it reached print status. All of this before I ever achieved my goal. Looking back over each project, I see it as the journey of working towards the goals that made accomplishing it so rewarding. Being **organized** is a skill, and not everyone has the skill, but they can obtain it through planning, preparation, and persistence. God wasn't just working on a book; He was working on me!

SHE'S UNSTOPPABLE because...

SHE *tends infallible, steadfast towards her goals knowing that she will be successful.*

SHE'S UNSTOPPABLE GOAL corner ...

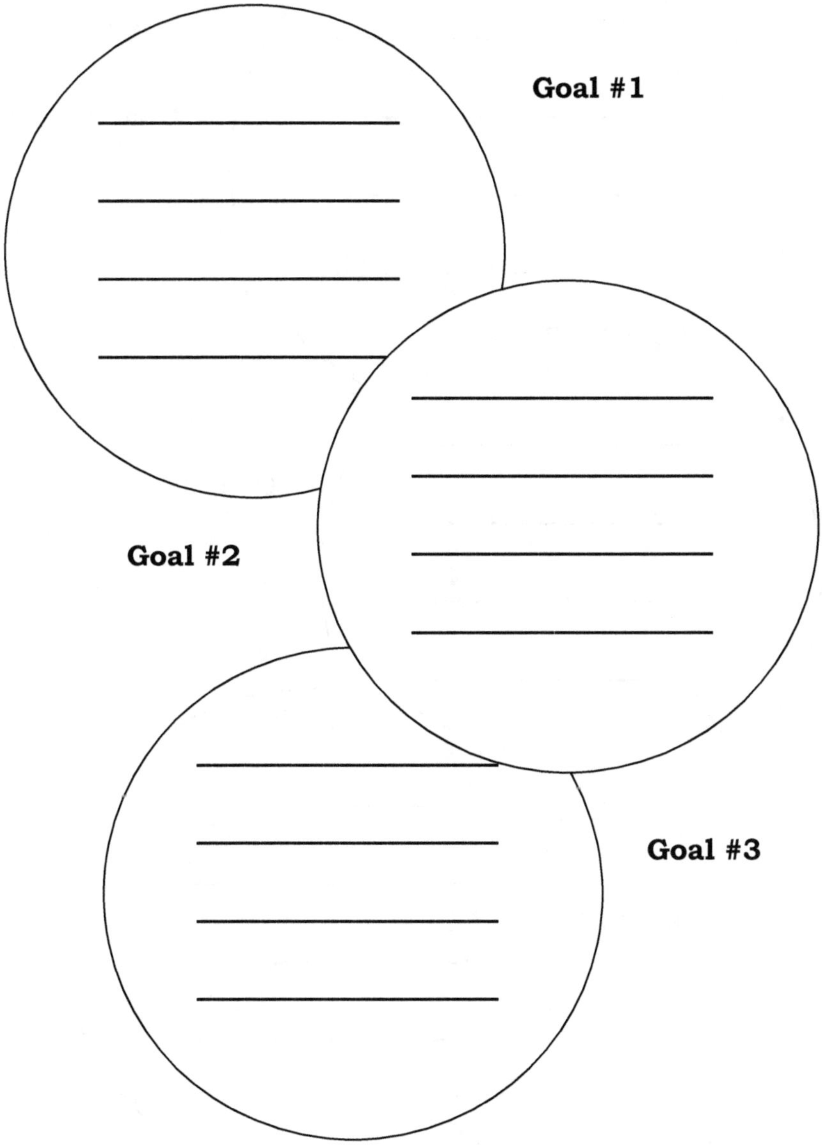
Goal #1
Goal #2
Goal #3

Micah Byrd

Goal #4

Goal #5

Goal #6

CHAPTER 5

SHE IS SUCCESS

What is success? Success can mean many different things to different people depending on who you are talking to. Webster's dictionary says that success is favorable or desired outcome; the gaining of wealth and fame; one that succeeds. I believe success is having the ability to pursue your own passions and purpose that has been planned for your life. I am successful, and so are you. I think and feel successful. I am able to make decisions on a daily basis about my earnings; I don't have to clock in or out to make those decisions. Most people go their entire lives with the hopes of being successful. When you make that choice there is no turning back. Ultimate success is having the power to write your own check, and being able to make changes to that check without having to ask for permission to do so. In this area of the book, I will share with you several ways that any woman can live a successful life. I promise that if you make these principles applicable and commit to doing the work you can live a one as well. I know these principles work because they have transformed my life causing me to experience prosperity, health, happiness and fulfillment in every area of my life.

SHE'S UNSTOPPABLE because...

SHE *is pursuing her passion.*

Being that your passions are the preview to your divine pathway for your life, your likes, dislikes, personality, motivators and interests are definitely not a coincidence. Identify your passions and pursue them by doing this , you will be taking the first step to becoming the successful woman that you were created to be. You should use your passions as a guide for success. Allow them to help you determine exactly what and where you want to go in life. Be sure to ask yourself these questions. What am I passionate about? What excites me? What moves me and gets my creative ambitions flowing? What do I look forward to? If I weren't consumed with financial obligations, how would I spend my time? You should journal these responses. Understand that your passions are your basic roadmap to follow.

Every moment that you can identify where something triggers excitement or flutters your creative ideas, you are discovering your purpose. This process came late in life for me, but I live by this principle now, and I am consistently flooded with ideas, inspirations, and innovations for my life's purpose. My passion is to share with women that **WE** can have it all, happiness, love, and success as business women. Because of that, I share with women how to balance the many roles that we take on. Even my love for fashion and accounting aren't by accident. It was purposefully designed for me. When I started my couture boutique, there were many people who told me providing high-end quality fashions would not work. They said that women are buying cheap clothing. I am still debating with them because I know that my target niche of women is out there and flourishing over the chic, luxury designs that the boutique sales. My knowledge of fashion is simply the hour-glass to assist me in teaching women how to live a fabulous chic boss life. There's not a day that goes by that I am not blessed in my ordinary activities of the day that stirs up my passions and guides me towards purposeful goals. Because of this, I wake up excited every day. I am excited every day about getting started with the tasks ahead of me. When I've organized my tasks and activities, I rest peacefully because I am satisfied with how I have spent my time. You too can experience this joyous way of living.

SHE'S UNSTOPPABLE because...

SHE *plans and prepares.*

We discussed, in the previous chapter, about being organized and its importance to being successful. Because your life should be planned on purpose, I start my day with a plan. I use daily to-do lists where I write down important tasks, phone calls, and appointments that will lead me closer to my purpose. Even if an instant fluttering idea sparks my imagination and I don't have the full concept of the idea, I write it on a post-it note and place it in a place that's visible. I will then transfer it to my list with the full concept and follow through.

Writing down your plans on paper allows you to crystallize it, making it something tangible that you can work towards. I love this saying "If you think it, ink it." Trust and believe that your thoughts are worth recording. With my daily to-do lists, I also write my plan for the month and year. This helps me see my upcoming events and appointments at a glimpse. With my monthly calendar, I mark important occasions like birthdays, anniversary, vacations, trips, book deadlines, speaking engagements, fashion shows, client's project(s) due dates, dates with my husband, events for my grandchildren, time with my adult children, personal time and appointments for myself. With a schedule as such, it is imperative to be in the know so that I am always prepared and never get caught slipping.

My best planning is having my personal relationship with my creator. It would be ultimately impossible for me to carry out such tasks without balance. I create space and time to have that personal dialogue with my creator because in those moments I am renewed, restored and recharged for the to-do-lists. Whenever, I am in the presence of my creator I am always seeking guidance, clarity and direction for my life, and day. When I leave out of meditation, I know that I am fully operating by a perfect plan for my purpose because I've allowed my creator to compose it.

Planning time for myself is important. I take myself out on dates. Or, I am known to go to a matinee movie on Monday's to see something of my choice. I also plan dinner dates for me on the days when my husband is at work or out with his friends. During these personal times, my imagination allows me to preview my greatness. I use this time to visualize projects or exciting things that I want to see take place. As these strategies arise within me, I immediately write them down and create a plan from that information and once implemented, the plans lead to the exceptional outcome I imagined.

Just as it is important to plan, it is equally important to be prepared. These two principles are synonymous. I've heard somewhere that you should "prepare for an opportunity that doesn't exist yet." You know that successful women expect opportunities to come and prepare energetically for them. I live by this principle in my personal and professional life. I am always planning to be the most prepared person when the next opportunity presents itself.

It is important to guard your time if you are going to be well prepared. It is imperative to protect yourself from things and people that don't deposit profitable dealings into your life whether that is monetized or informational. The scripture says [13] "She makes sure her dealings are profitable, her lamp burns late into the night." Any plan you initiate for yourself becomes worthless if you don't have the time to work on it. It is imperative to guard your time with diligence. Select your appointments and engagements wisely. You must not feel guilty about protecting your time. It is a precious commodity that you have, and once it is spent, you will never get it back. It is unsettling for me to be busy throughout the day and still have not accomplished anything on my to-do-list. I am extremely unsettled with wasting my time on senseless engagements, and people if there is no direct correlation to what I am doing. I am flexible with my schedule because there are times when impromptu events will happen, but I don't allow it to take me off course. I am not afraid of saying NO especially if I am spreading myself too thin or allowing others to distract me from what's important. Time is imperative, and we all are given the exact amount of time every day. What will make the difference in

---

[13] Proverbs 31 v 18

your success is how you choose to use your time. So spend it wisely!

SHE'S UNSTOPPABLE because...

SHE *who wakes up and finds herself at the top has not been asleep.*

SHE'S UNSTOPPABLE because...

SHE is OPTIMISTIC. *To be successful, she must first believe a successful outcome for her life. You can take this to the bank "you get what you expect."*

SHE'S UNSTOPPABLE 109

The scripture says [14] "She is clothed with strength and dignity, and she laughs without fear of the future." You know that your expectation acts like a faith magnet that will pull you in the direction of your expectation – be it positive or negative. It is a principle found in the Bible. You are sure to attract whatever you are, so make sure that only great things are operating on the inside of you. Every day there's a choice that you can make, whether that is being happy or sad, smiling or frowning, laughing or crying. It is a matter of your choice. I am truly what my astrological sign says, that I am someone who sees the glass half-full versus half-empty.

I, like other successful women, simply choose to be optimistic. I have a habit of making it easier, so choosing happy, smiling and laughing suits me. I know the enemy gets very upset when my feet the floor every morning. I can just hear

---

[14] Proverbs 31 v 25

it saying "darn did she just got up again after yesterday's obstacles." When challenged with a choice whether to laugh or cry, I'd rather just laugh because no problem, circumstance or setback is greater than my creator. I make the choice to turn those situations over, and I go about my day expecting that all is well.

There is nothing better than adversity. ***"I don't chase anything I choose"***! I had to shed a lot of unnecessary stuff to gain the blessings that we're trying to get through. I do believe that we live in a universe that creates based on energy. Biblically speaking this world was created because words were spoken.

ENCOURAGMENT TIPS

- Optimism pays, and pessimism will cost you if you are going to be successful. There has been research completed indicating that happier people get compensated more, promoted faster and more efficient and successful than their pessimistic counterparts. This is because optimistic people seem to think that things will work out, so they take more risks and end up succeeding because of their thoughts.

- In regards to negative, pessimistic people have a difficult time keeping their jobs, friends, and relationships. Their fearful and faithless outlook to life beseech the negative results they fear in the beginning. They definitely get exactly what they expect. Don't you just loathe hearing the response from a negative person, when you say "hello, how is your day?" You are sure to get a negative comment from them, so for those individuals, it is always nice and much more pleasant to just say hello and have a super fabulous day. Pessimism will keep you from sowing, which will keep you from harvesting. Break the cycle of negativity. Even if you are not a natural jovial individual by personality, you can still learn how to be a shining optimist. The scriptures say [15] "When she speaks, her words are wise, and she gives instructions

---

[15] Proverbs 31 v 26

with kindness." Here are some principles I use in my own life to keep me optimistic and focus on the brighter side.

- Greet the Day Expecting Only Good.
- Banish Negative Thoughts Immediately.
- Confess Your Way to Optimism.
- Become Your Own Biggest Cheerleader.
- Lighten Up and Laugh
- Surround Yourself with Optimistic Individuals.
- Catch Someone Doing Something Right.
- Eradicate Fear, Doubt, Jealousy and Mistrust.

In order to be successful, you must live in pursuit of something. You must be willing to pay the ransom in order to achieve your goals. Success will always escape people that spend their time looking for a quick way to propel. People with zero goals are always wishing for achievement and have no real plans to get there apart from hoping that one day they will wake up and find that their circumstances have changed. You can never expect to accomplish success if you are spending your time on nothing else other than planning for the weekend movie, the party you are going to attend or the television show that you plan to watch. There is absolutely no cheap discount for the cost of success. If you spend your time pursuing leisure rather than fulfilling purposeful goals, you will end with a disaster.

Now, don't get me wrong there are times that you just need to unwind from your hustle and bustle. I suggest that you spend those times with meaningful things, such as reading a book on what will assist you with your next goal. Take a trip that is enlightening or helps expands your outlook for that next project. Get your family to engage outside of the box by including them in different things that they have never tried. You will be surprised how doing these things will help you open up creatively.

It was once pointed out about the tragedy of the once powerful Romans. At one time, the Roman Empire was the greatest nation the world had ever seen. Yet, it was invaded and destroyed not by the Goths but by the circuses, luxuries, and indulgences that made the once tough people soft. Even though the Romans worked extremely hard to build a very affluent society, they grew soft and lazy after conquering the world. The people craved for ease, free bread, the circuses and easy living. Just about one out of every two days was a time of leisure. Case and point, Rome, under Nero, celebrated 176 legal holidays each year. Instead of setting forth to explore new horizons, the people focused on leisure and lost their will and drive to live. The government became their benefactor, and their sense of purpose was lost. In the end, their great society was conquered and destroyed.

Disappointing, history hasn't really taught us anything different. Many women today are still caught in the trappings of **goal-less** living. They would rather listen to the news than make news themselves. They would rather watch television than read a book. They would rather sleep than think. People without goals are not productive, yet they want what achievers have. Break out of this way of life. If you want the higher life, you can't reach it with low-level living. Set purposeful goals. Even while I was writing my book I was attending online graduate school for my master's degree. You can't be lazy with those many projects and goals happening around you.

Here are some really easy ideas for setting and achieving great goals.

- Set goals **prayerfully**.
- Make your goals **motivating**.
- Make your goals **specific**.
- Put your goals in **writing.**
- **Create** actions plans for your goals.
- **Set** a motivating reward.
- **Look** at your goals **daily.**

Once you implement these ideas and take action, you will ascend towards success. If your life has become lackluster and boring, chances are you either lack goals, have lost sight of them or need to reevaluate and set new ones.

Be a woman of prayer. A successful woman is a spiritual woman. There is no lasting success apart from success in God, through God and with God. A woman's prayer life is the foundation of the success habits that are written in this book. When a woman's prayer life is in intact, so is her success. I know first hand that when your prayer life is shaky, inconsistent or non-existent, then success will yield the exact results shaky, inconsistent or non-existent. I have experience that success and failure in life can be traced back to your prayer foundation.

SHE'S UNSTOPPABLE because....

SHE *starts her day and ends her night with prayer.*

Finding a quiet place to pray. My quiet place for prayer is my shower. But, it can be your bedroom, car, shower or study just as long as it's your place free from distraction.

Finding time to pray consistently. When I lost my way and my prayer life started to slip. I noticed it was because I was consistent with praying. And, when I implemented a schedule for my prayers instantly things begin to change. So, don't get caught up in the time of day you pray, just as long as you make if part of your daily routine.

Taking time to listen. A prayer is a form of communication, which means you must take the time to listen after you have spoken. Spend time talking to God, but allow Him to talk back to you. It's smart to record what He says to you in your prayer journal. His responses are worth noting.

Pray the Word. God's provisions are in His Word, so pray the promises that you find in His Word over your life and they will come to pass - **2 Corinthians 1 vs 20**. **Pray in faith.** When you pray, **believe** that you received what you are seeking. God wants to answer your prayer and give you exactly what you have asked for – **Matthew 7 vs 7 – 8; John 14 vs. 14, 16 vs. 23 – 24; Mark 11 vs 22 – 23**. After praying, make a faith gesture. Behave as it the answer is on its way because it is!

Pray persistently and fervently. Don't give up on the power of prayer – **James 5 vs 16 – 17, Luke 18 vs 1 – 8!** The power of prayer will open doors, provide your specific needs and incite success in all your endeavors. I always pray before I go into business meetings and I receive the very favor and results that I prayed about. My prayer life increased when I decided to start my business. It during my prayer time that I heard the still voice say "it was time for me to step out on faith" regarding the specific prayers for my business. **Prayer changes things!**

Pray, your desires. Don't be afraid to pray for "things" God wants to give you the very desires of your heart, and He knows that many of these desires include material things. I always pray for God to bless me with clothes, shoes, and nice things, and I get exactly what I've asked for. Ask for what <u>you want</u> and believe you receive it and you shall have it - **Mark 11 vs 24, Psalms 37 vs 4; Matthew 6 vs 25 – 33.**
Doing these things and making prayer your lifestyle, you will flourish in spiritual and natural things. **It is one of the habits for success!**

Visualize your future outcome. My type of learning style is noted as **visual.** I am a visual learner because I prefer using images, pictures, colors and maps to organize information and communicate with others and myself. It's easier for me to visualize objects, plans, and outcomes in my mind's eye. And, many years ago I realized that there was power in visualizing your future. When you imagine and rehearse your God given dreams on the inside, they will come to pass on the outside. I have done this myself and the results were exactly what I visualized. I always devote time to godly meditation, but years ago I receive divine instructions on how to effectively mediate. It's known that in the bible God always gives "faith props" to people so they would visualize their future outcome.

- God gave Jacob a witty idea for both himself and the cows to visualize spotted stalks so they could have spotted off-springs (Genesis 30 vs 36 – 39).
- God gave Abraham dust, sand and stars so he could visualize how many descendants he would have (Genesis 13 vs 16, 15 vs 5; 22 vs 17).
- God told Joshua to look at the city of Jericho and visualize sweatless victory over the inhabitants (Joshua 6 vs 2).
- God showed Peter a vision of wild animals to reveal to him that Gentiles could reccive the gospel too and that he should take the gospel to a Roman officer (Acts 10 vs 10 – 16).
- God showed Jeremiah an almond tree, a boiling pot and a pillar in a vision and used them as faith props to get him to see how He was going to use him in ministry (Jeremiah 1 vs 11 – 19).

The more I practice this principle of visualization, the more I see it work out in the lives of successful others. I am convinced; your imagination is truly the dress rehearsal so you can be the star on the stage of Life. Studies show that when you rehearse something in your imagination, your mind registers it as if you are really doing it. God designed your faculties so you could see beyond your present circumstances and have hope for your future. God has so much success planned for you, but you must begin seeing it in your imagination through the eyes of faith before you can act on it. What you meditate on, you will attract. Your subconscious mind will register what you have visualized and begin to work in cooperation with the Holy Spirit to force you to do the things necessary to bring it to pass in your life.

I've seen it happen too many times in my own life, for your to convince me that it doesn't work. Your mind, imagination and spirit are the tools God uses to bring about His ultimate success in your life. Release your imagination over to Him. Let Him fill it with visions of new possibilities for your life.

Visualize beyond your paycheck. Do it

right now, it won't cost you anything to dream. Set aside a day this week, one hour to do nothing but visualize and dream. Pull out your journal, planner or even a board and cut out words, pictures, and phrases that inspire and encourage you. Put together at least one whole page. Then sit back and ask yourself some questions. Why did those things speak to you?What new direction, idea or priority is God trying to reveal to you? See yourself having **extreme success.** Visualize yourself living in the best home, owning the best vehicle and having the best marriage and family. See yourself partaking in luxurious vacations and wearing the finest clothes. What does it feel like? Sound like? Smell like? Look like? Now open your eyes. That is what your life is supposed to be like in God. You **can** live a fabulous life!

Your imagination is a preview of your life coming attractions. As you pursue success God's way, **expect** to encounter and experience the very things you have visualized. There's nothing too hard for God, it's all a matter of the faith pictures working on the inside of you. If you can see it and believe it, you will receive it! Visualize your way to an incredible life, **I did! It is one of the habits for success!**

Maintain an exercise routine for yourself. The number one killer of success is a lack of energy and poor health. I personally know in my own life that if I didn't maintain an exercise routine, I would not be able to keep up my vigorous pace and pursue purpose to the magnitude I do now. The physical stamina and endurance that is required to accomplish high levels of success are **only** achievable through properly conditioning your mind and body with exercise. Studies show that people who exercise have better attitudes, higher self-esteem, self-confidence and higher sex drive needed to achieve their daily goals. Exercise is also known for improving the quality of your sleep, makes your mind and focus sharper and strengthens your body. When I begin exercising it was because I wanted to be fit and in shape. I wanted to keep myself tight. Now, I do it as a way of life. I know that if I am going to be successful in life, I must have a healthy and energetic body. Although I am tired sometimes and I don't feel like exercising, I resist the temptations of skipping exercise. I might not do the full out routine on those days but I will get a full exercise of cardio. I know it challenging creating positive habits and it easy to create bad habits, so I stay away from the temptation to slack. I will immediately put away what I am doing, get dressed like a firewoman and begin my workout routine. This habit eliminates all excuses and sabotages slothfulness so it will not sabotage me. My health is important to me and it's not work playing around. In my younger days, when my children were young. I prepare myself for a morning run, every day during the week. I would see them get onto the school bus and immediately after the school bus would pull off I would run my 5 miles. It was the most exhilarating experience I would have. I received my most creative and electrifying ideas during those times. The bottom line is this: if you want to be around to fulfill your purpose and enjoy success in life, you must do everything in your power to protect your health and exercise now. Here are some encouraging tips to get you on the move.

Determine to make exercise part of your daily routine. Make up your mind whether you want to exercise in the morning, at night, or in the middle of the day. Some women like to exercise first thing in the morning to give them the extra pep in their step for the day while others find it more convenient to exercise on their lunch hour or right after work. Whatever you decided, **just decided!** Find a time that suits your work, and lifestyle and commit to exercising at least thirty

minutes to an hour a day, three to four
times a week.

Make exercise fun. If you find an activity
that you enjoy, your chances are greater
at being committed to it. There are several
exciting and thrilling activities that you
can do to exercise. My favorite is
rollerskating. But, there is aerobics
classes, karate, kickboxing, hip-hop dance
moves, Zumba or another favorite of mine
is walking my dog. Incorporate some fun
factors to your routine by mixing it up to
keep things exciting and keep your body
confused with the type of exercises.

Get educated about exercise. I am an
advocate on enlightening yourself for the
knowledge. And, learning about exercise is
no exception to my rule. I have subscribed
to multiple health and nutrition
magazines to refine my understanding of
my body and refresh my personal health
philosophy. I want to stay in the know on
the latest exercise tips and tricks. Reading
provides you an ample amount of
encouragement you'll need to get you
going.

Do double duty. Use your exercise time to
get caught up on some reading. Listen to
some motivational audio tapes, watch
your favorite television program or even

catch up on some reading. It's surprising the number of things you can do while exercising. I've done some projects, caught up on my magazine reading, wrote notes for pending projects all while exercising. Time is important so I always make the most and the best of it.

Set a motivating exercise goal and an exciting reward. Having an exercise regiment without a reward is discouraging. Even if your not trying to lose weight, challenge yourself to lift more weight, run faster, or simply do extra sit-ups. Goals will give you a specific point to target your **faith** and help you track your progress more effectively. Along with a tangible goal, create a tangible reward. Reward your progress with a new workout outfit, a day to the spa or whatever you find personally fulfilling. You were created by God to be reward orientated, so take advantage of your make-up by finding a carrot to dangle at your fitness finish line.

Get appropriate fitness partners. Stay away from people who will talk you out of your fitness goals or constantly pull on you to keep them motivated. Because of their lack of personal discipline, it will drain you of your resolve. Instead, partner up with someone that are just as committed to their health as you are to yours. I recently linked up with a trainer so I wouldn't be solely accountable to myself for results. I know that the primary benefit of a personal trainer is having an encouragement coach that will push you farther than the effort that you would normally give on your own. With my trainer checking on me and demanding progress, my motivation has quadrupled significantly. I haven't always been in the position financially where I could afford a personal trainer, but it didn't stop me from doing what I could to exercise on my own. At the end of the day, how fit you are is strictly personal. Don't expect everyone to join your pursuit for extraordinary health. You must make that decision for yourself.

If you focus on nothing else, remember this one thing: the hard work of maintaining an exercise routine *does* pay off. It may not be today, and it might not be tomorrow, but it will happen, so feel confident and maintain your exercise regimen. **It's one of the habits of success**.

SHE'S UNSTOPPABLE because...

SHE knows the importance of her health, it is the difference between survival and just making it.

Be Consistent. Success is not automatic. It definitely requires that you put forth a consistent effort in order to obtain it. There are too many women waiting for God to make them successful when He clearly stated in His Word the need for you to *make your way prosperous* by taking action on his Word (Joshua 1 vs 8). God needs your **faith** and *consistent* action in order to bless you. Learn to become consistent.

I have multiple areas in my life that I focus on being consistent in order to maintain the high level of success that I have.

Be Consistent in Your Efforts. I know that diligence is the key to increase and opportunity, so I daily do the needful things to guarantee that I complete all assignments and meet all my goals on time. This might be the reason for my anal behavior of being driven by my deadlines which my continued effort gets the job done. Writing books is always a lesson in consistency. It takes consistent effort to meet the due date. Often time if I put the book down even for a day, it can derail all my efforts. Instead, I stick with it and write unceasingly – day and night – but the rewards are always worth it in the end! Changing lives one book at a time is a priceless treasure in my life.

Be Consistent in Your Thought-Process.
Don't allow your thinking to slip to the point where you get off the Word. No matter what comes up against you, make sure you consistently stand on the promises of God. I always use the overcome in every area of my life.

Be Consistent in Your Prayer and Planner. I am convinced in the power of prayer and godly meditation so I make using my prayer and planner a regular way of life. There's not a week that doesn't go by that I don't write in my planner, illustrate ideas that I have in my planner and there's not a day that goes by that I don't pray over the things I have put in there.

Be Consistent in Making Time for Yourself. Let me tell you that "ME-TIME" is necessary. It is important to my mental well-being. I can't possibly give out to everyone else, without creating a reserve bank of self-care and love within myself. The best gift that I can give myself is some *retail therapy.* Find something that you delight in and pamper yourself consistently.

Be Consistent with God. Be consistent in your prayer life and bible study. Prayer should be a daily practice and Bible Study should at least be weekly. Direction, comfort, encouragement and even correction from God are invaluable to the success journey.

Be Consistent with Your Family. In the business of life, don't lose sight of quality time with your family. Be there to consistently communicate love to your husband and children. Schedule regular date nights. Spend time daily talking and listening to your family. Lasting success begins in the home, so keep these relationships well tended.

NOTE: *I can earnestly share this with you because you all know that I **almost** lost my way with my husband. I stop being available to listen, and our date nights begin to drift way. I am so grateful to the voice of God!*

Be Consistent with Your Standards. Don't slack when it comes to your image and integrity standards. There's never an off-season when you can let these two critical areas go. Live a life of moral excellence and maintain impeccable image regardless of the circumstances that will come to challenge you. Maintain your consistency at all costs.

Be Consistent with Your Purpose. It takes time to become an overnight success. Don't get weary in well doing (Galatians 6 vs. 9). Due season always comes! Stay the course and be consistent no matter what and you will reap a multitude of rewards.

When looking to develop a life of consistency it is important that you avoid destiny detours like competition, comparison, and laziness. Competition and comparison break your focus and will rob you of your blessings. Instead of sticking it out until your season comes, competition and comparison will cause you to jump off your bandwagon and on to someone else's. God created you to run your race. Stay focused on your assignment and you will get the fruit of your assignment. Equally, avoid the temptation to be lazy. Success requires diligent effort and there are many mundane things you must do on the way to doing what you love. Stick it out and always give your best all the time.

If you master consistency in these areas and avoid the destiny detours of competition, comparison, and laziness, you will excel in life, just I have. **It's one of the habits for success.**

Be Mature. Maturity, like success, doesn't come without a price, yet its fruit is priceless. Mature women are readily apparent. We stand out in a crowd and display a cool, calm and confident demeanor even in the worst experiences. They exude strength and stature and attract the attention and recognition of successful others. Mature women seem to handle challenging situations and people with ease and consistently get the results promised in the Word of God.

If this sounds too good to be true, it's not. You can be a mature woman. It defined in the webster's dictionary that **maturity is "state of being fully developed".** Ephesians 4 vs. 11 – 13 discusses maturity and development that derives from being under godly Pastors and leaders. Paul writes, "And he gave some apostles; and some prophets; and some evangelists; and some pastors and teachers; for the perfecting *maturing* of saints...Until we all come in the unity of the faith and of the knowledge of the son of God, unto a perfect *mature* man, unto the measure of the stature of the fullness of Christ." A great way for you to mature as a woman of God is to join a ministry and place yourself under the teaching of a good pastor. Good pastors will instruct you how to mature according to the Word of God and serve as a role model for you. Maturity is a process and it does take time, but there's no better time for you to jumpstart your development than right now.

Below are five key attributes that depict how mature woman think, acts and operates. Follow this example and you will develop well-formed maturity in you.

A Mature Woman Lives by the Word of God. As it pertains to matters great or small, your decision making should rest on the principles and promises found in the Word of God. Never make decisions based on your own feelings or personal opinions. In its place, let the Word of God shine on your path and instruct you on what to do and you will succeed every time.

A Mature Woman Refuses to Tolerate Drama. Don't give ear to the drama queens in your life. They will weight you down with gossip, complaints, and criticisms if you let them. Refuse to let their small issues and small talk keep your life and mentality small. Eliminate their influence by surrounding yourself with successful others who walk by faith.

A Mature Woman is Patient Under Pressure. Tests and trials come to everybody, but only the mature pass the test for success. Make up your mind that you won't fall apart under adversity. Learn how to be patient and poised when the heat is on, and what God deliver you and give you sweat less victory.

A Mature Woman Operates in Excellence No Matter What. Never play hit or miss in your own personal or professional excellence. Consistently give your very best to your spouse, children, boss, mentors and ministry, regardless of what you might feel like, and you will inevitably rise to the top.

Take a minute to evaluate yourself. Have you been thinking or acting childish lately or have you been making progress towards a mature self? If you set your will to grow up, you will **go up. It's one of the habits**

for success.

Be A Finisher. One of the habits in my life that have helped me tremendously is that of finishing what I start. It doesn't matter if I am starting a new workout routine, engaging in or working on something with my grandchildren, I set my mind to finish before I even begin. Successful people are finishers. We tackle projects with the will and attitude that we won't stop until we succeed. We see the finish line before we get there. As a result, we become **unstoppable.** W achieve success after success after success. Regardless of the challenges, we keep on winning.

That is how I have always lived my life. Before I ever achieved any notable amount of success I purposed in my heart to be determined to fulfill God's will for my life. I know that whatever God has given me to do, He's already given me the grace to finish it, so I operate with this mindset. I have emulated this attitude for years, people who have the opportunity to be around me adopt this same spirit.

In order to accomplish this successfully, I have created my "Extreme Team". This is a small group of women that have a finisher's mentality and will do whatever it takes to get the job done. That can mean working around the clock with little to no sleep to complete a project or kicking into overdrive to meet a deadline, we set in our minds that we will **not quit** until we finish. Because we possess this mentality, we achieve extraordinary results. For example, when I was writing this book , I was also attending school online working towards completing my second Master's program. There were many late nights and early mornings. If you're going to succeed at your God-given goals, you must develop a non-quitting attitude. People who don't quit get promoted, receive favor and experience accelerated success.

Quitters, on the hand, give in to negative reports, challenges, and make excuses for why they can't succeed.

Achievers on the other hand simply figure out a way to finish despite the obstacles. Beware of a quitter's mentality.

Prepare yourself to go the distance and finish strong by:

Counting Up the Cost. Evaluate what time, talent and resources it will cost you before you get started. A clear vision and plan is the first step to completion.

Gathering Your Tools. Make a list of items you need to be successful and then go out and purchase them. Don't be too cheap to invest in your own success.

Confessing Your Completion. Speak your way to your goals. Say positive words like " I can do this" and "I am going to finish strong". What you confess, you will possess. Don't give any voice to your complaints, frustrations, or challenges. Instead, speak only faith for your finish.

If you do these things you will blast past barriers and overcome all obstacles to fulfill your God-given dreams. Become a finisher. **It's one of the habits for success.**

Keep Your Words Right. Learn to maximize speaking the right words. You can talk your way into a mediocre life or a maximum life by speaking **LIFE** over yourself. Read about the children of Israel in Numbers 13. They forgot to keep their words aligned with the Word of God and as a result they spoke themselves right out of the blessings of God. Their report was full of words that spoke doubt and unbelief which kept them from entering into the Promised Land.

Remember the old adage says "Loose lips sink ships." Never speak out of your initial reactions to a situation. Formulate the right words for the response that you want to see based on the promises contained in the word of God. Then confess words of life, faith, victory, power and success. What you confess you will possess.

Be alert of your words in common conversations. This is usually the time when most women mess up. They take too lightly their conversations on the phone, a chat with their co-worker or a heart-to-heart with their girlfriend and end up saying the wrong things.

Words such as "I'll never get over this." or
"This is killing me." will come flying out of
their mouth and trigger the very results
they want to avoid. Don't allow this to
happen to you. Train your mouth to speak
life-giving, faith producing words. Develop
a confession for success and you will have
it .

I live by the principles. I have a confession
for every area of my life including my
purpose, family, my faith walk, marriage,
ministry, and prosperity. I carry them
around with me on a **SHE'S
UNSTOPPABLE** notepad, so I can say
them throughout my day. As I confess
them in faith believing God, my words act
like magnets to draw my desires to me.
Confession is a power principle found in
the Word of God. I believe in this principle
a lot that I want to equip you to start
putting it to action in your life today. As
you've read the pages in this chapter of
the book, you've now encountered sixteen
habits for success.

It is my prayer that each of these habits
become such a part of you, that it
transforms the very course of your life and
propels you to success.

To begin your life-changing journey, I have made it simple for you by writing a 'Success Habits Confession' that you can use to speak these habits into your life. As you make this confession daily, the Holy Spirit will begin to prompt you to take action on your words. Obey the prompting and begin to move in faith to do the things you confess. Your words partnered with your faith action will draw you to your destined end of success.

SHE'S UNSTOPPABLE because...

SHE *knows the power of her next move is all in what she speaks over her life.*

If you confess it, you will possess it. **It's one of the habits for success.** Say this confession aloud now.

SUCCESS HABITS CONFESSION

Dear Heavenly Father,

Your Word says in Mark 11 vs. 23 that if I don't doubt in my heart, but instead believe that those things which I say shall come to pass, I shall have whatsoever I say. Therefore, I confess theses sixteen habits in my life and believe that I receive them now.

Next projects and goals...

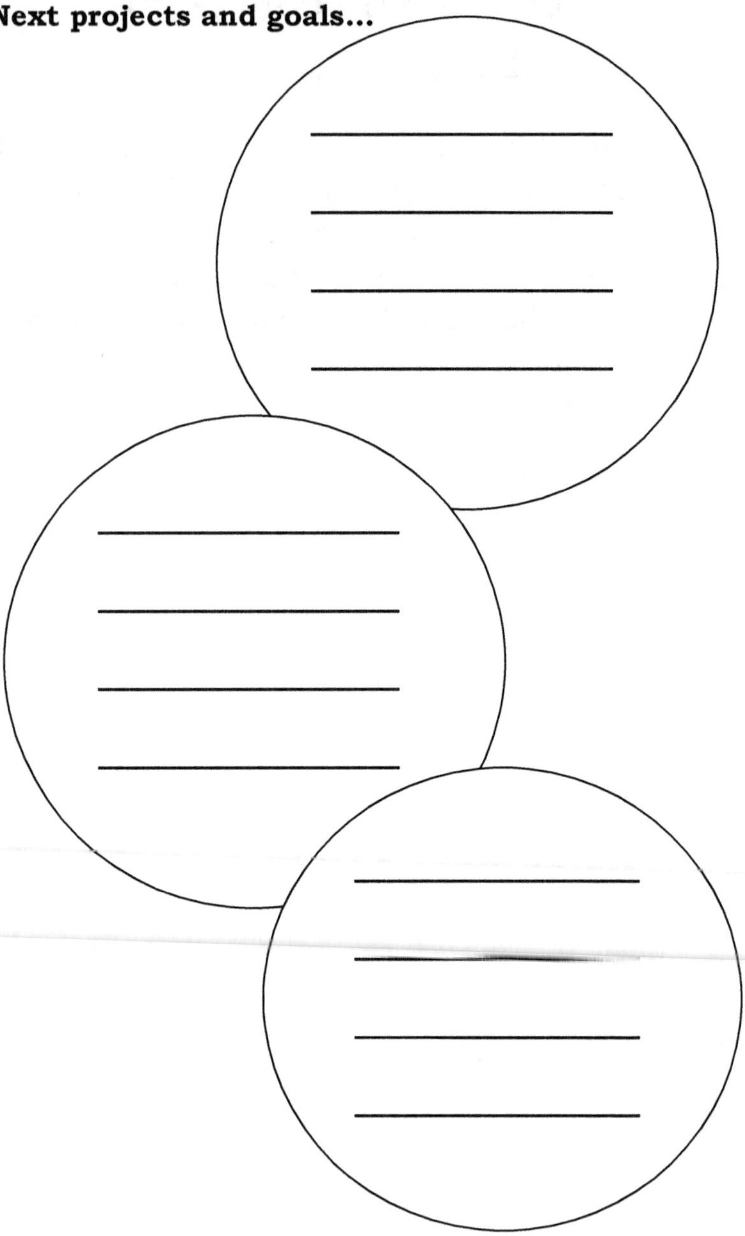

CHAPTER 6

ABOUT HER BUSINESS

The scripture says [16] "She is energetic and strong, a hard worker." [17] "She makes sure her dealings are profitable, her lamps burn late into the nights." A day, moment nor thought goes by without me reflecting on my day's encounters. Starting a business isn't easy, especially if there are no systems in place to operate the business. I quickly learned that my experiences with establishing goals, vision boards, and lists afforded me the understanding of implementing systems for my business

---

[16] Proverbs 31 v 17
[17] Proverbs 31 v 18

and personal. I accomplish my best results when it's written. Let me explain, when I developed the bookkeeping and tax company I knew there was no one within my reach that I could emulate to make my experience easier. When I first started the company I would go into my office every day like I had a calendar booked with clients to serve. It was those days that I would create systems and policies to help me and my staff, the staff I dreamed I would have developed structure for the business. There were times when business was slow and I had to supplement my income to offset the revenue the business wasn't generating. So, I did odd jobs like paper delivery, security, nurses aide and more. Those odd jobs I would get were always completely different from my main gig, which was my bookkeeping and tax business. I didn't want to burn myself out with providing those services for some other established business and work on building my business at the same time. Because I wanted to remain focus and fresh for my clients that I was beginning to build by implementing my systems and policies in the practice. An Accounting Firm isn't a new business but I definitely tapped into a niche' that wasn't being served. So, I wanted to capitalize on that by providing consumers what they were missing. I noticed that consumers in relation to the tax industry services where the primary tax companies were H&R Block, Jackson Hewitt, Liberty Tax, and other new companies were only open from January – April. I made sure that my clients and potential clients knew our services were provided year-round. I also educated my clients and potentials that we provide assistance with addressing notifications from agencies such as Internal Revenue Service, and local municipalities for prior year tax filing. Upon opening my accounting and tax practice, I noticed there was a huge disparity for people with tax issues. Many of those issues were due to the tax payers own accord but it was a concern for a large group of individuals and they needed assistant addressing them professionally. Which lead me to notice some other issues that had a major impact on tax preparation, and that was bookkeeping service being provided accurately and consistently prior to the tax preparing. So, I started offering packages that included bookkeeping and tax preparation for individuals. Since I am a public accountant this service was a bonus for my clients and potentials. When I would attend networking events, my peers would say, "oh, you only offer bookkeeping services?" The amount of business that was being unaddressed confirmed to me that even during a difficult economy my business will withstand. I absolutely didn't see those comments as an insult. I enjoy servicing my clients in this fashion. I have had multiple years of exposure and experience in corporate America, working with top executives and major corporations. I prefer exactly what I am doing to this day!

When I decided to add another venture to creating multiple streams of income. I wanted it to be something that is close to me, that identifies with me inside and out and so a women's retail boutique was my dream. I have provided accounting services for this industry for a number of years and the back office structure I was fully educated about; however, the front operation of this industry intrigued me especially since fashion is my passion. This was a venture that I had no one to emulate. So, with many of those practices and systems that were created in my first business, I implemented those with some tweaks to fit the industry. The retail industry is difficult and with no assistance, it has been a major hurdle to accomplish. I did reach out to another boutique owner to try and form an alliance, but because women are so intimidated by other successful women, her ability to extend a helping hand wasn't offered. Therefore, I became competition for her establishment and many other boutiques in the surrounding area. I didn't set it up to be that way but due to my experiences being a direct impact on my initiation it happened. I would always say every morning to my children when they were little, that 15% of their day is based on others remarks, but 85% is based on their response. In essence, what I wanted them to learn early on is that we are always in control of the outcome.

My boutique provided uniqueness and quality to our consumers it begun drawing the competition customers when the word got out. My boutique, my perspective was definitely different for this region of Georgia. Most consumers in the area were accustomed to traveling downtown Atlanta to get designs and styles that my boutique provided in their own area, south outside of the city.

Throughout history, women have always ignited social, economic and cultural trends and movements. There are more women who pursue entrepreneurship and experts are declaring that there is no better time than right now for women to be in business. They have observed and is reporting how we are redefining the business model on our own terms "Women business owners have change the face of business," both literally and figuratively. With that being said, the face of women's entrepreneurship is also changing as more women of color enter into this arena. Conventional wisdom says that we EntrepreneuHERs have a bright future and addresses if we have what it takes to be our own boss, follow the step-by-step process to turn our idea into a viable business, and work our plan. Success for small business is well within our reach. Trust and believe that there is definitely wisdom in the cliché "If it was easy, every woman would be doing it." EntrepreneuHERs get straight to the point when we are asked, "If starting a business is difficult and risky and definitely not for the faint of heart."

Running your own company means you are responsible for **everything** in the operation, and at the end of the day, we are the "throat to choke" especially during the start-up phase. Understand that as you get up and running and begin to find your groove, you will become synonymous with your business, making it a top priority in your life, planning strategically which will assist with balancing the many hats that we all wear whether you like it or not.

Having no formal training in tax preparation (i.e. tax law) when I started the firm back in the 90s, there were definitely many learning curves. I had no idea exactly what services and to whom I would provide those specific services to during that time. It wasn't until several years later after working with my white counterparts that I learned there was a huge disparity between what their clients were educated on and what my clients were informed about. I have made it the firm's mission to educate people about tax laws rights and how to save money with deductions and credits via tax codes issued by the regulated authorities.

I didn't know that owning an accounting firm would bring me many nights of disappointments and some huge laughs at the same time. Truthfully speaking I have heard some wild stories, but I enjoy what I do. It brings me joy to enlighten individuals on the true and honest reason why paying taxes is suggested. The primary reason why the accounting and bookkeeping service is the staple piece for the firm is because you cannot understand your true net income without knowing what your revenue and receipts are on a monthly basis. Yes, you better believe I educated my clients on tax laws and rules that will benefit them with tax dollar savings.

So, why do you want to be an EntrepreneuHER? For me, there are benefits and rewards to the risk-taking woman with the vision to start a successful business. Although making money is the primary incentive for going into business in the first place, let's talk about something else for a moment. Do you remember that specific day, time and moment when you decided that you were going to be your own boss? Do you remember when you decided that you were **no longer going to run that rat race?** Do you remember whether or not it was an idea, a circumstance(s) or just the mere inclination that it was time to begin that business? Well for me it was that moment 'when my back was up against the brick wall", that moment where I had been working for one of the top 500 Accounting & Tax Assurance companies in the world i.e. KPMG Peat & Marwick for many years. Yes, the pay was great. I was a six-figure earner and was loving life with my kids. I felt like I had made several sacrifices in my life and it was time for me to relax and enjoy some of the fruits of the labor. Right before going into the meeting for my review, I took a deep breath and prayed the 23rd Psalms, you know the one that says, [18]"The Lord is my shepherd, I have all that I need. [19] He lets me rest in green meadows" he leads me beside peaceful streams... my mother has always instilled this prayer within me to recite when I am feeling uneasy, or when anxiety is trying to creep in. Being self-sufficient was something that I privately imagined. I imagined it on my own terms and time.

SHE'S UNSTOPPABLE because...

*Every day **she is** turning her dreams into her drive.*

---

[18] Psalm 23 v 1

SHE'S UNSTOPPABLE because...

SHE *understands that power in agreements add value to what* *she* *does i.e. friendship, relationship, and business arrangements.*

SHE'S UNSTOPPABLE 110

I had not planned and my women's intuition had been nudging at me before to get my stuff in order, and I knew it. I internally knew that time was drawing near because one day it was "review time" and before this time I'd never received a bad review on my work performance and I absolutely didn't see onc coming. I was always at work on time, all of my accounts were balanced to the penny, and if not there was full explanation documented made in the disclosure notes but this particular review felt different. On the day of the review, I honestly didn't feel good and for some odd reason, my stomach had the largest knot in it that I literally thought something was severely wrong with me. Let's just say, that when the "spirit" wants to put a word inside of you, it definitely knows how to get your attention. Be careful what you process because you just might get exactly that.

It was that infamous day, the day of my review when I was informed that my position was being relocated to Texas. Just after I'd purchased my first home for my three children and me. I was devastated and distraught because I was unprepared but I had the option to follow the position or step out on the given opportunity and, that's exactly what I did. I decided to begin my own accounting & tax firm providing services to a larger business community yet small in reference of categorization. I have not looked back since!

SHE'S UNSTOPPABLE because...

SHE *knows faith doesn't make it easy; faith makes it possible!*

My entrepreneurHER experience has helped me grow so much, in more ways than I probably would have if I had remained employed in my corporate career path. Let's talk about those adversities. As a woman, our lives are a balancing act. Yes, I said it, and there's no other gender that can balance life like us women. We strive to create a successful business; manage a household; be a great wife, mother, girlfriend, and confidant; and still squeeze time to pursue other interests. Where exactly in the business plan should we write, "Get to my cycling class two times a week", or "Take my husband out for a date on Wednesday"? because Lord knows, men scream for their attention in many different ways.

Where is it taught to handle the many rejections notices received from the bank when you're attempting to get that loan for business infused cash flow, or creditors ringing your phones off the hook. Where is it taught to handle your kid's school play happening the exact night you have a client's project due or the night your husband wants some attention because you've been on your phone?

SHE'S UNSTOPPABLE 111

Define balance for yourself and prepare for your entrepreneuHER journey. With the efforts of being very clear and knowing what's important in our lives, let's prepare a mental mood board that assesses our lifestyle and provides an understanding of this EntrepreneuHER journey. It is what I call the **"M"** factor:

1. (Peace of) MIND
2. MONEY
3. MARRIAGE and / or MOTHERHOOD
4. B(M)W (or whatever is your "motor vehicle")
5. MORTGAGE

You can arrange this list how you see fit for your lives. This is just what resonates with me because when my (peace of) mind is affected due to my money circumstances not being alright, my marriage and or motherhood abilities are affected, which will cause me to lose my BMW and my mortgage (home). There will be others that you can add; however; the point is to know what's important in your life to prepare to be that successful entrepreneuHER because eventually, you will come to a point of the pre-determined boundaries of protecting and balancing your M factors. The time will come when you will have to decide if it's best for you to keep going or if it's time to tell yourself "I did my best, and I'm done." The failure of your business does not mean you're a failure as an individual. Even if you fall flat on your face, that is forward motion, progress, and opportunity to learn. I know you will take that experience and parlay it into your next entrepreneurial venture, approaching the new opportunity as a much smarter and wiser person who will know exactly what it takes to be successful. Me deciding to temporarily close and relocate my boutique came as an unfortunate disappointment to me but based on my initial financial projections and promises of my upscale location and good demographics; I thought business would be profitable by the time we reached the six-month mark. Despite the on-going, positive monthly marketing, advertisements, critical acclaim, customers who loved us and daily social media postings, the business was taking too long to reach profitability and was losing too much money. The retail business pulls on customers' discretionary income and in my case, that income was apprehensive. The research had been done and despite being in this upscale location these consumers had gotten accustomed to what was provided to them which was the local outlet center, and the second-rate shopping mall.

Having an execution plan in place affords me the opportunity to move on to my next journey. The boutique is now an online business that is doing really well in sales. I have successfully minimized a large portion of the overhead costs that incurred monthly.

But since I enjoyed providing high-fashion styles to women, don't count me out because **I will be back** with a twist to retail "where exclusivity will meet the everyday woman."

CHAPTER 7

SHE'S UNSTOPPABLE!

1. She is her own cheerleader!

2. She is not fooled by those experiences dressed up as distractions because she knows "life is 10% of what happens to her and 90% of what she does about it!"

3. She understands that power in agreements add value to what she does i.e. friendship, relationship and business arrangements

4. Every time SHE thinks about giving up on herself, she reminds herself of her WHY.

5. There are times in her life when she feels she just can't keep going, then she remembers all the other times

SHE has made it through.

6.   Behind every one of her experiences, there will be a lesson and a blessing. She MUST wait on both of them.

7.   SHE tends infallible, steadfast towards her goals knowing that she will be successful.

8.   SHE is pursuing her passion.

9.   SHE plans and prepares.

10. SHE who wakes up and finds herself at the top has not been asleep.

11. SHE is OPTIMISTIC. To be successful, she must first believe a successful outcome for her life. You can take this to the bank "you get what you expect."

12. Every day she is turning her dreams into her drive.

13. SHE knows faith doesn't make it easy; faith makes it possible!

14. SHE starts her day and ends her night with prayer.

15. SHE survives.

16.   SHE understands that power in agreements add value to what **she** does i.e. friendship, relationship, and business arrangements.
17.   SHE knows the importance of her health, it is the difference between survival and just making it.

18.   SHE know the power of her next move is all in what she speaks over her life.

About the Author

Micah Byrd is the owner of MICAH BYRD Bookkeeping & Tax Service a boutique Accounting Firm, and BYRDS Couture an online boutique that has a fashionable presence in Atlanta, Georgia.

A graduate of Strayer University, with a Bachelor of Science in Accounting, and her MBA with Entrepreneurship as her concentration from Capella University.

Micah has been a business owner for twenty-three years. Her experience comes from her multiple consulting partnerships, where she has been instrumental in launching and implementing solid financial platforms. She has worked for many known Fortune 500 companies. Her business highlights are providing accounting structure for start-ups and seasoned businesses.

She is the 2010 "Entrepreneur of the Year" winner awarded by (GMEN) Georgia Micro Enterprise Network and she was also awarded the "Excellence in Sustainability Awareness. This award pioneered Micah in implementing *going green initiates into* her accounting practice for her clients. Micah has been marked by many of her clients as providing a service that "**gets down and dirty with the numbers**". Her niche is the forensic process of accounting and tax preparation.

She has been dubbed for not appearing as a Public Accountant because her style proceeds her skills and knowledge, but Micah Byrd is very well known for her intellectual aptitude when it comes to her profession. Born and raised in Atlanta, Georgia, she is the wife of a loving and supportive spouse, the mother of three college graduates, and the grandmother of two beautiful grandchildren, a daughter, sister, dog lover, and an advocate SHOPPER.

www.ingramcontent.com/pod-product-compliance
Lightning Source LLC
LaVergne TN
LVHW051246080426
835513LV00016B/1761